Where a leaf never dies in the
still blooming bowers,
And the bee banquets on thro'
a whole year of flowers.

Guest stationery of the Naples Hotel, 1904

DEDICATION
*To the memory of my father, Aaron I. Sanson III, and to my mother, Nancy S.
Sanson, whose unselfish support and love inspired me to explore the world
around me and gave me the courage to take the risk to tell the story.*

Photo: Nanette Sanson

IN PORTRAIT

NAPLES

AND COLLIER COUNTY

EDITED BY

NANETTE S. SANSON

PROFOLIO EDITIONS INC.

NAPLES, FLORIDA

Photo, facing page: As the sun descends, flocks of birds begin to head south of the
Naples pier to quieter sections of beach or to the rookeries opposite Key Island and
Marco Island, where they will converse throughout the evening hours.
Photo: Nanette Sanson.

CONCEIVED, EDITED, AND PUBLISHED BY:
Profolio Editions Inc.
5020 Tamiami Trail North, Suite 200
Naples, Florida 33940

PUBLICATION UNDER THE DIRECTION OF:
Nanette S. Sanson, President and Editor-In-Chief

PHOTOGRAPHY EDITOR:
Nanette S. Sanson

BOOK AND COVER DESIGN:
Jennifer Schumacher and Natalie Coté,
Schumacher Design

SENIOR TEXT EDITORS:
Elizabeth Cameron and Patricia Finlay

PRODUCTION DIRECTOR:
Nanette S. Sanson

COVER PHOTOGRAPH:
Naples Pier by Nanette S. Sanson

BACK COVER PHOTOGRAPH:
Birds in flight by Nanette S. Sanson

EDITOR'S PHOTOGRAPH:
Diane Bélanger

CAPTIONING:
Introduction, Lifestyle, Nature by Nanette S. Sanson
Architecture by Andrea Clark Brown with Kris Paradis
Arts and Culture by Nanette S. Sanson with Kris Paradis
The Heartland by Janina Birtolo and Kris Paradis
Our Natural Heritage by Nanette S. Sanson with Dr. John H. Fitch

Color separations by Palace Press International,
San Francisco and by Groupe 5, Montreal.

Printed and bound in Quebec, Canada by
Imprimerie Interglobe Inc.

Library of Congress Catalog Card Number: 95-74826

ISBN 0-9648108-1-6 (Hardcover)
ISBN 0-9648108-2-4 (Paperback)

Printed in Canada
First printing, November 1995

Photo, right: Nanette Sanson

A C K N O W L E D G E M E N T S

The publisher wishes to acknowledge the following individuals for their unwavering faith in this project and for their generous support without which this publication would not have been possible:

Monique Girouard
Hal LaPine
Martyn and Elizabeth Pummell
Robert M. Reed II
Nanette S. Sanson
Mary A. Vincent
Suzanne P. Williamson
Frances L. Wolfson

Many people have extended extra efforts to assist in the completion of this project. The publisher would like to specially acknowledge the following for their professional contribution and inspiration:

CREATIVE SUPPORT:
Andrea Clark Brown
Elizabeth Cameron
Myra J. Daniels
Jennifer Deane
Dr. John H. Fitch
Susan Heydt
Deborah Levinson
Kris Paradis
Nanette S. Sanson
Jennifer Schumacher
Eric Strachan
Carl J. Thome

MARKETING AND ADMINISTRATIVE SUPPORT:
Michael Batchelor
Diane Bélanger
Ann Burnham
Patricia Carpenter
Sally Fitch
Rosemary Hobert
Aaron I. Sanson IV
Dawn Sanson

COMMUNITY AND CONTENT CONSULTANTS:
Ann Allen
Peter Van Arsdale
Barron Collier Company
Kay Bullington
Collier County Museum
Dee Dee Cox
Bolton Drackett
Tim Hiers
Marissa Hartington
Mayor Paul Muenzer
O.B. and Tina Oceola
Diane Patterson
Dr. Robert Read
Redlands Christian Migrant Asso.
Dr. and Mrs. Leslie Schultzel
Miles Schoefield
Michael Watkins

The editor wishes to thank, in particular, Nancy S. Sanson and Robert M. Reed II, whose encouragement, thoughtfulness, and almost daily contributions throughout the project have given a very special meaning to the realization of this book.

My parents and grandparents moved to Naples in 1946. Although we would not be considered a "founding" family, we have been actively involved in the community for three generations. Growing up in Naples in the mid-1950s and early 1960s was great.

One of the things which made Naples special during those years was the way so many citizens gave unselfishly of their time and resources to build the community. Parks, roads, water-treatment plants, and the pier are all examples of the services and facilities which were built during that time and which formed the base for what many today call "quality of life." The planning and zoning for the older part of town are a tribute to the foresight of the city's leaders. Everyone worked together to make the necessary improvements. There was truly a united community.

I often tell people that I was born in Fort Myers, since there was no hospital in Naples then. It seems to surprise them. There were no Boy Scouts and only six Little League teams until 1965. There was still only one high school until 1972. I look back on those times with appreciation for the things we did have.

Most of my early summers were spent at Cambier Park where I played baseball with friends in the mornings, tennis in the afternoons, and organized baseball in the evenings. Sometimes, I would umpire or keep score and report on the results for the old *Collier County News.*

I can remember when First Street (Gulfshore Boulevard) ended at the Naples Beach Club. I also have fond memories of Sundays after church when the family went by boat to the beach at Marco for a picnic. That was before the Marco bridge was built and it was very quiet with no-one else around. We'd dig a hole in the sand and build a fire to cook hot dogs.

Since the 1960s Naples has grown very fast. Ironically, the real stimulus behind that growth was the financial boost the area received from insurance settlements after Hurricane Donna blew into town on September 10, 1960. Today Naples is quite different from what it was when I was a kid. We should be thankful, I guess, that the early expansion of the town occurred in a fairly organized fashion—in major east/west swaths from the Trail to the beach, starting with Coquina Sands, the Moorings, Park Shore and, more recently, Pelican Bay. My dad used to tell me that he and others named the streets in Coquina Sands by sitting around with books on local shells and trees.

From my perspective, it is hard to love Naples today the way I did when I was growing up. From a business standpoint, things are generally good, but, from a personal standpoint, I'm concerned that we may be killing the goose that laid the golden egg. Swift and continuous growth has placed a tremendous strain on the attributes of the area that brought everyone here in the first place.

I know nothing stays the same, but it is my sincere hope that we can manage change in a way that respects the fragile and essential balance between population and environment.

One thing is clear: each of us can still make a difference in Naples and in all of Collier County by taking on responsibility for the future. Each voice can be heard and each individual can contribute. It is often difficult for new residents to gain a clear picture of the problems we face. Creating a consensus on major issues is a challenge due to the disparity in the way newcomers and old residents measure priorities.

Collier County, which is wonderfully diverse socially, environmentally, economically, and culturally, has few equals. It is my hope that we will all work hard, as the early citizens did, to keep it that way.

Michael Watkins

At Delnor-Wiggins Pass S.R.A., the one-mile long beach provides a magnificent
environment for an early evening stroll.
Photo: Nanette Sanson.

Life in Southwest Florida hangs in a delicate balance. One of the most ecologically unique areas in the continental United States, this region is home to a singular blend of tropical and temperate zones. Sea and land come together in a dynamic convergence of rich nearshore ecosystems, mangrove forests, and coastal barrier islands. Coastal estuaries and broad, shallow bays create a link between inland wetlands, cypress swamps, and upland pine flatwood forests, providing one of North America's most productive breeding grounds for fish, shellfish, and other forms of sea life.

Today nowhere are these magnificent natural ecosystems more intact than in Collier County. Comprising some 2,000 square miles, the region is a treasure house of flora and fauna that have benefited from its geographical location and from farsighted conservation efforts. Florida's Southwest Coast had the historical good fortune of being "discovered" later than the eastern and northern regions, and during the last thirty years, nearly fifty percent of the land in Collier County has been put aside for conservation.

Thanks to Florida's landmark conservation legislation—Preservation 2000—the U.S. Fish and Wildlife Service, the National Park Service, the Florida Department of Environmental Protection, the Florida Forest Service, the Florida Game and Fresh Water Fish Commission, and local Native American tribes have all become active conservation land managers and participants in ecosystems conservation in Collier County.

The Florida Panther Refuge, the Fakahatchee Strand State Preserve, the Big Cypress National Preserve, the Ten Thousand Islands Preserve, and the western region of Everglades National Park—a wetland of international importance—have all benefited from their efforts. These ecosystems not only maintain biodiversity, environmental quality, and natural resources for the present, but constitute an invaluable legacy for future generations.

Despite these successes, native landscapes and ecosystems are threatened as never before by the demands of expanding human population. Collier County's population of nearly 200,000 people represents a doubling of population every decade since the 1950s. Demographers forecast that population in this fragile natural environment will reach 250,000 by the end of the century and as many as 500,000 by the year 2020. Can Southwest Florida accommodate this increase without detriment to its natural environment and quality of life or will it come to resemble Southeast Florida's urban complex?

One thing is certain: if strong efforts at conservation are not maintained, the only subtropical landscapes and ecosystems still intact in the continental United States will vanish forever. Gone will be the region's unique species of plants and animals, environmental quality, and its very rich natural resources.

Ongoing conservation efforts cannot succeed unless the citizens of Southwest Florida and officials at all levels of government appreciate the value of what is at stake, understand what must be done, and are prepared to act. Acquiring and protecting Collier County's environmentally sensitive lands will require public awareness, understanding, support, and participation.

There is every reason to hope that Collier County will respond to future challenges as it has in the past. If it does, it will continue to serve as a model for people all over the world who understand that by ensuring the conservation of the rich diversity of natural life, they not only improve the quality of human life but help guarantee its survival.

Dr. John H. Fitch

The palm islands in the middle of the savannahs in Big Cypress National Preserve form a perfect backdrop to the fall colors of the marshes. These wetlands preserve the fresh water table which is necessary to support increasing populations.
Photo: Nanette Sanson.

The exact moment of inspiration is as difficult to pinpoint as it is to seize upon perfection at its prime. It was sometime during an early morning stroll along Naples beach that the idea to publish a pictorial story about the area that I have grown to value so dearly first captured me. Over the following eighteen months, it was my fascination with recording the many facets of nature and of the spirit of Collier County that carried me forward. I did not entirely contemplate the complexities of publishing a book until it was too late to stop. It has been a journey of discovery, wonder, and satisfaction. I would not now dream to trade a single moment.

There could easily be as many words as pictures to describe my experiences and my awe of the diversity and beauty of the natural and man-made environments that are found in every corner of Collier County. However, I felt that a visual poem would be the best way to reflect the events and sights that renew one's spirit time and time again as one experiences this unique area.

There is so much to see and do in Collier County that it would have been impossible to include everything in this book. The 200 images, which were chosen from the over 10,000 considered, were selected to encourage further exploration of this land and its mysteries, traditions, and natural treasures.

This documentary portrait attempts not only to underline the many challenges facing Collier County, but also to address the contrasts that have always defined the region. It is a picture of interwoven threads that have bound together nature and man, urban and rural communities, and protectors of the environment and proponents for economic growth into a web of discourse for more than a century. This book portrays many of the ecosystems that are struggling to survive the pressures of population growth, the people and the traditions that have made every community unique, and the flora and fauna that serve as a constant reminder of just how delicate and precious the balance between man and nature really is.

Collier County is a region in transition. There is still something so intimate and simple about the spirit of life in the area, due in large part to the powerful presence of nature. The glitter and growth has been held at bay by the wise decisions concerning planning, zoning, and preservation that have taken place over the last forty years, and which continue to challenge conservation and community leaders today. These efforts and the incredible environmental legacy bestowed on Collier County have made it one of the most desirable and unique areas in which to live in the U.S.

The question of how commercial and residential growth can be stimulated without sacrificing or destroying the present quality of life and the precious natural ecosystems to which the economy and culture of the region are so profoundly linked continues to challenge Collier County. Fortunately, there is still a chance for community leaders to find solutions which will ensure a shared vision of a sustainable future for both the natural environment and the way of life so valued by resident and visitor alike.

This book is not intended to find solutions to these problems but rather to share those aspects of lifestyles, cultural traditions, and our natural heritage that are worthy of preservation. Maybe our future is reflected in the past. I hope that the links between the past and the present portrayed in this book will help others understand the importance of the work being done by conservation groups, community organizations, and civic leaders as they consider the legacy of the past while planning for the future.

During this project I have been moved by the synchronization of birds, mesmerized by the rhythms of the sea, awed by the fragility and primal beauty of the Pehheoke—the River of Grass—in the Everglades, and energized by the enthusiasm of the people whom I have met in this very special region of the world. For all of this, I thank you Collier County.

Nanette S. Sanson

The sun rises through the mist, illuminating a man-made canal in Golden Gate
Estates. These canals along and passageways under the I-75 highway permit water
and wildlife to move through the Everglades.
Photo: Nanette Sanson.

Facing page: Gordon Pass separates Naples from Key Island, a seven-mile long coastal barrier island to the south. *Above:* Marco Island and the Isle of Capri rest surrounded by the Gulf of Mexico and the mangrove forests of the Ten Thousand Islands.
Below: Representing two very distinct lifestyles, the high-rise condominiums along Park Shore offset the individual homes in the Moorings.
Photos, facing page: Carl J. Thome; top and bottom: Gilbert Booth.

LIFESTYLE

Collier County lies along the southwestern coast of the Florida peninsula, embraced on one side by the Gulf of Mexico and on the other by the Everglades. Geographically, the county is larger than the state of Delaware yet its total population is less than 200,000. The landscape, where nature is a constant presence, is as diverse as the people. Stretching from the shoreline to the hammocks of the interior, Collier County encompasses some of Florida's most elegant communities, most productive agricultural lands, and most spectacular natural preserves.

For more than a century, Collier County's coast has served as a winter playground of the well-to-do. The residents of the interior's small towns and barrier islands—ranchers, farmers, fishermen, and Native Americans—have, by contrast, retained traditional ways of life. From Old Naples to the most isolated towns of the interior, the people celebrate a spirit of community. Throughout its vast reach, the county is a haven

Facing page: Washed by the warm turquoise waters of the Gulf of Mexico, Collier County's coastline of over 25 miles of unspoiled white sand beaches and thousands of protected barrier islands is one of the most alluring in the U.S.A.
Photo: Kimberly A. Bell

LIFESTYLE

for wildlife species, including alligators, panthers, and bald eagles. This interplay between man and nature has resulted in some of America's most beautiful golf courses and planned communities, which keep company with some of nature's most extraordinary preserves.

One of the last areas of Florida's coastline to be developed, Collier County was protected both by nature and history. For decades, mosquitoes and swampy land discouraged all but the most determined of settlers. Aware of the high-rise sprawl that transformed the East Coast, Collier County has ensured from the first that development was consistent with the quality of life treasured by its residents. The result is a testament to their forethought: a lush community of landscaped boulevards and well-planned developments along the coast and a rich mixture of farmland, reservations, and nature preserves in the interior.

Considered one of the last frontiers, each community in the county boasts eccentricities as delightful and various as those of any frontier region. Life, then and now, was based on a close relationship with the land and the sea. These were the constants: land sharks and carpetbaggers came and went. In the early 1900s, settlements

centered around hunting and fishing. Communities such as Goodland, Ochopee, and Everglades City arose as supply posts and push-off points. Everglades City was selected as the county seat by Barron Gift Collier, for whom the county was named, and in 1928, the first government building was erected there. However, Everglades City did not prosper and the county seat was moved to Naples.

Naples is probably the most recognized community in the county. The city may have been named from early advertisements trumpeting its charms as the "Italy of America." Throughout this beautiful city, waterways and manicured golf greens dominate the landscape. There are more golf courses per capita in the greater Naples area than any comparable area in the world.

Old Naples, in the historic section of the city, retains the essence of small-town life. Its residents seem to move at a more leisurely pace than in other parts of the city. The sense of community that exists in Old Naples is reinforced by its historic atmosphere. Its tree-lined streets are flanked with quaint cottages and the coastline remains uncluttered by high-rise condominiums and superhighways. Visitors are frequently awed by the day-after-day perfection of the winter weather. Year-round residents enjoy the daily drama of flashing summer storms that sweep suddenly out of the Everglades and disappear as quickly into the Gulf of Mexico. As the storms pass, a rainbow-hued bouquet of hibiscus, bougainvillea, and oleander glows in the sunset.

Positioned in the Gulf of Mexico with the Ten Thousand Islands at its feet, Marco Island is largely a community of boaters. The development-by-design of the island began in 1964 and the people who have since settled there are simultaneously more urban and more island than the rest of Collier County. Canals run inland from the coast, creating a backdrop for many homes. The canals crisscross the island to form an aquatic lacework for islanders to dock and pilot their boats.

Those who seek solitude settle farther inland. In Golden Gate Estates, folks tend their horses and walk in their own wooded acreages. Although many of these estates are private residences, others use the land to raise a variety of livestock as diverse as cattle, llamas, and ostriches. These people live their own brand of frontier life.

Agribusiness rules in northeast Collier County. Tomato fields and citrus groves stretch to the horizon. These fields and groves produce enough food to rank the county near the national top in the production of fruits and vegetables. Immokalee is the hub of this activity. Its population rises and falls with the reap-and-sow rhythm of the fields. Immokalee has the feel of a border town with its wide streets, Spanish street signs, cultural festivals, and

migrant population. Here, Mexican, Haitian, Guatemalan, and African-American cultures blend together, creating the unique spirit of this community.

Throughout the county, people pocket themselves around nature preserves and other protected lands in usually unnamed neighborhoods. One of these communities is located near Corkscrew Swamp Sanctuary in the northeastern quadrant of the county. Here, people do not measure their amenities in terms of golf courses, restaurants, and shopping centers; rather they appreciate the cypress woodlands, which they share with otters, ibis, and gopher turtles. The solitude is occasionally punctuated by the cry of eagles returning to their nests.

Collier County well deserves its reputation as a winter resort. There are many fine hotels, shops, restaurants, and cultural offerings and the magnificent weather allows visitors to enjoy a daily variety of recreational activities, as well as the natural treasures of the region's nature preserves.

This subtropical canvas displays a unique palette of lifestyles—from traditional ranch life to the life of leisure—and in Collier County, the number of choices is exceeded only by their quality.

Rick Compton

The best part of the day for a fisherman or woman begins at sunrise. As friends pursue the "big one," the pleasure of the sport is surpassed only by the joy of their camaraderie.
Photos, top: Eric Strachan; bottom: Nanette Sanson.

18

A full moon setting at sunrise over the Gulf of Mexico is as beautiful as the sunsets
that draw hundreds of visitors each evening to the 1,000-foot long Naples Pier.
Photo: Nanette Sanson.

As an early morning mist lifts over the beautifully landscaped Grey Oaks Country
Club, a golfer addresses the day's first challenge. Many of the more than 50 golf
courses in the Naples area are renowned for their award-winning designs and
sensitivity in preserving existing natural areas.
Photo: Carl J. Thome.

Collier County's seashores come alive in the early morning as people enjoy a ritual
stroll along the beach in Naples and shell fishing on the sandbars around Marco Island.
Photos: Nanette Sanson.

Opportunities to enjoy Collier County's wilderness areas are abundant.
Above left: Visitors to Clam Pass Sanctuary explore the bay and mangroves by boat or
by trams provided by the Registry Resort. *Above right:* A swamp walk in the
Fakahatchee Strand Preserve is one of the many activities of the Briggs Nature
Center. *Below:* Corkscrew Swamp Sanctuary is a favorite with bird-watchers.
Facing page: An airboat ride in the Everglades provides a spectacular up-close look at
its scenery, wildlife, and birds.
*Photos, top left: Registry Resort; top right: Nanette Sanson; bottom: Cara L. Jones;
facing page: John J. Gillan.*

Sophistication and luxury aside, it is the strong community spirit in towns throughout
Collier County that enriches the quality of life for residents and visitors alike.
Photos, top left: Eric Strachan; top right: Nanette Sanson; bottom: Lance Murphey.

The eclectic mix of cultures and lifestyles in Collier County is as diverse as
its natural treasures.
Photos, top: Tim Stamm; bottom left: Cara L. Jones; bottom right: Eric Strachan.

Collier County's commitment to educational excellence has placed its schools and students in the top ranks of state performance scales. *Above:* Children enjoy their graduation ceremony from a Head Start program. *Below left:* Students of the Community School benefit from the low student-to-staff ratios for which the county is recognized. *Below right:* Edison Community College expanded to a new 50-acre campus in Naples in order to meet increasing demands for higher education. *Photos, top: Eric Strachan; bottom left and right: Kenneth White.*

A winning home run captures yet another championship game for the Naples
Chiefs. National girls' softball has never been the same since teams from Naples
began a winning streak over 15 years ago. The famous Naples Braves have won an
unprecedented seven consecutive Senior League World Series titles.
Photo: Eric Strachan.

"Just another day in paradise" is a phrase often heard in Naples. Collier County's
subtropical temperatures, which rarely fall below 70 degrees F, and the lulling rhythms
of the Gulf of Mexico are irresistible lures for lovers of boating, bathing, and fishing.
Photo: Nanette Sanson.

Boating is the *raison d'être* for many who live in or visit Collier County. While the
bounty of the Gulf attracts fishermen, the warm Gulf breezes offshore entice sailors.
Photo: Kim Weimer

Naples is known as the "Golf Capital of the World." *Above:* The Club at Pelican Bay
is the centerpiece around which an entire community has been established.
Below: Collier's Reserve Country Club sets a new standard for design and land
management practices. It is the world's first Audubon Signature Cooperative
Sanctuary course and preserves 130 acres of wetland and forest that provide habitat
for a variety of wildlife. *Facing page:* The signature hole at Lely Flamingo Island Club
is proof that public courses can be as challenging as private ones.
Photos, top: Nanette Sanson; bottom: William C. Minerich; facing page: Carl J. Thome.

Throughout Collier County festivals and events mark each month of the year.
Above: Driving through "Mile-O-Mud" track, the Swamp Buggy Races in Florida
Sports Park in Naples captivate fans from March to October. *Below:* The Great Dock
Canoe Races held in May are Naples' oldest annual community event.
Photos, top: Lance Murphey; bottom: Nanette Sanson.

The International Horse Trials is one of many philanthropic endeavors which benefit communities in Collier County. The proceeds from the two-day equestrian event are donated to help support the children of Immokalee.
Photo: William C. Minerich.

As the sun begins its descent to the horizon, a lone fisherman enjoys the tranquility
and beauty of Delnor-Wiggins Pass S.R.A. in Vanderbilt Beach.
Photo: Nanette Sanson.

Children delight in the numerous recreational activities available to them
throughout the day.
Photos, top: Nanette Sanson; bottom: Carl J. Thome.

Above: From the quaint atmosphere of Tin City to the European charm of The Village on Venetian Bay and the historic sophistication of Third Street, the variety of choice for shopping in Collier County is full of unexpected pleasures. *Below:* The fine arts have always received special attention in Collier County. More than two dozen art galleries in Naples showcase the works of local, national, and international artists.
Photos: Carl J. Thome.

From Vanderbilt Beach to Marco Island, favorite seaside chickee bar/restaurants
provide the setting to enjoy the end of the day. The Vanderbilt Inn on the Gulf is
one of several spots along the coast with an "Old Florida" atmosphere where one can
relax and watch the sunset.
Photo: Nanette Sanson.

Residents and visitors gather on the lawn of the Naples Beach Hotel and Golf Club
to enjoy the free concerts of the "Summer Jazz on the Gulf" series.
Photo: Jennifer Deane.

The town of Goodland, near Marco Island, offers a special taste of good-old "down county" fun. *Above:* The Buzzard Lope Queens take center stage at the weekly Sunday gathering in Stan's Idle Hour Lounge. *Below:* The sign at the Old Marco Lodge Crab House indicates that a visit to Goodland is indeed a very memorable experience.
Photos, top: Cara L. Jones; bottom: Nanette Sanson.

Opening night at the Philharmonic Center for the Arts held in November marks the
beginning of a whirlwind season of cultural and social activities in Naples.
Photo: Carl J. Thome.

Early evening light bathes the lounge at the Ritz Carlton as another magical
Southwest Florida night begins with "cocktails at the Ritz."
Photo: Ed Chappell Inc.

Above: The breathtaking sunsets of Southwest Florida often draw applause from those who gather along its shores to witness nature's spectacle of color.
Facing page: Concluding another perfect day, the *Rosie,* an authentic 104-foot Mississippi River paddlewheeler, cruises into the sunset off Marco Island.
Photos: Nanette Sanson.

ARCHITECTURE

Collier County showcases the rich variety of the historical and contemporary architecture of Southwest Florida. Whether built for civic, commercial, or residential purposes, the buildings in the county are frequently defined and enhanced by their natural setting. Beachfront, waterway, hammock, or woodland are among the county's diverse natural environments which lend a special aesthetic environment for its architectural treasures.

Communities in Collier County are dedicated to preserving their architectural heritage. Fine examples of historic properties can be found throughout the county, including Everglades City Town Hall, the old post office in Ochopee, the Roberts Ranch in Immokalee, and Palm Cottage and the Keewaydin Club in Naples. The "Old Florida" rustic or craftsman styles of many historic properties in the area continue to influence contemporary design and renovation.

The history of settlement in Collier County can be traced through the evolution of its architecture, from its most

Facing page: Bridging the gap between old and new, the Bay Colony Club uses beams and rails to re-create an "Old Florida" look. Arched doorways and interior windows provide a Mediterranean flair. Architect: David Humphrey. Built 1991.
Photo: Jennifer Deane

rustic beginnings, epitomized in the design of the Smallwood Store in Chokoloskee, to the monumental postmodern Naples Philharmonic Center for the Arts.

Everglades City Town Hall, one of the first civic buildings to be built in the county, was set in a prominent location overlooking the village green. Its placement is a prime example of urban planning that ensured that this beautiful colonnaded Neoclassical structure dominated its surroundings. Unencumbered by decorative landscaping, the building stands on its own, giving it authority as the hub of the city's official business transactions.

Many of the oldest buildings in Collier County were built in the "Old Florida" styles. Fine examples of this rustic design are the Rod and Gun Club in Everglades City and the Keewaydin Club on Key Island in Naples. The three-story, white clapboard Rod and Gun Club still retains its historic charm and elegance. One of the lodge's most impressive architectural features is its long wooden verandah, which overlooks the Barron River. This fishing and hunting lodge features an original tin-stamped ceiling and walls panelled in pecky cypress, on which are hung

memorabilia of the early days of Everglades City and the famous people who have visited the club.

Visitors to the Keewaydin Club will find that little has changed since it was built in 1935. The main lodge still retains an old Florida ambience with an oversized fireplace in the main hall and a restaurant and reading rooms which look out onto the beach. The modern cottages that were built on the club's grounds in more recent years have been carefully integrated with native trees and plants.

Collier County's earliest residential architecture includes homes built in the "Old Florida" craftsman style. Palm Cottage, built in 1895, is a prime example of this style. This 12-room house was constructed of "tabbie"—a type of mortar made from local oyster shells—and is the only tabbie home remaining in Southwest Florida. Palm Cottage exemplifies the layout of the houses of its era. They were built to take advantage of natural sea breezes. Attention was paid to their orientation to the sun so that light could flow from one room to the next. These dwellings often had high dormers or upper story windows and an open living room or stairway area that vented the interior during hot, daytime hours. Glass transoms in the bedroom doors permitted both light and air to enter rooms on the upper floors. Although elementary design features, these thoughtful elements are seldom used in contemporary air-conditioned residences.

Architecture in the heartland of Collier County reflects the special value placed on the land. Ranch styles predominate even to this day. Roberts Ranch in Immokalee remains a remarkably intact collection of historic structures, which depict the architecture of an early South Florida ranch. The estate, the site of the first ranch and orange grove in Collier County, represents over 100 years of history.

"Firmness, commodity, and delight" have long been considered characteristics of great architecture and these attributes are evident in Naples in the overlay of street trees thematically organized by neighborhoods on an east/west, north/south grid. Whether leaning, columnar, heavily draped, or brightly colored, these alleys of trees create a neat and beautifully structured pattern of nature's riches placed under command by the city's insightful forefathers. Most of the downtown tree planting took place in the 1950s. Today these mature trees provide a striking counterpoint and delightful balance to the variety of Old Naples' residences, supporting a very special and eclectic blend of home types not possible in other areas of Collier County.

The courtyard plays an important role in the architecture of Naples. This prototypical open space is elaborately employed in both public and private realms.

The most notable public courtyards are picturesque exterior rooms found in commercial areas such as Waterside, Third Street, and Fifth Avenue, and the numerous "half courts" along the streets and avenues of Old Naples. Also distinctive is the Venetian Village, where courts and sidewalks become indistinct yet powerfully marked with public art and gathering places.

Commercial architecture styles in Collier County span from Neo-Mediterranean influences to the postmodern style represented by the monumental Naples Philharmonic Center for the Arts. Set amid the natural beauty of Pelican Bay, the Philharmonic Center is in total harmony with its surroundings. Although the building dominates the cityscape, it proudly displays the fact that modern architecture need not be intrusive but rather can add a new and inspiring look to a city that takes pride in its past.

Though style and construction techniques change with time, sunlight and rain will always be a part of the equation. Use of spectacular views and integration into the subtropical landscape will always be there too. Each of the special problems and opportunities that Southwest Florida's climate has to offer gives architecture here a unique and ever-changing face.

Andrea Clark Brown

A Neoclassical pedimented porch adorns the facade of Everglades City Town Hall, the original county seat. Its deliberate location as the focus of the town square makes it a true example of early urban planning. Architect: William O. Sparklin. Built 1928.
Photo: Kimberly A. Bell.

Restrained and elegant, Trinity-by-the-Cove Church in Port Royal is a simple
structure of primary geometric shapes. The perfect placement of its windows ensures
a constant wash of daylight within its interior. Built: 1958.
Photo: Jennifer Deane.

The interior of the historic Palm Cottage, the second oldest home in Naples, exemplifies the special attention paid to the Florida climate. The architectural design allows sunlight and sea breezes to ventilate the entire house. Its tabbie mortar structure makes it a distinctive landmark. Built: 1887.
Photos: Jennifer Deane.

Third Street South in Old Naples offers up an eclectic mixture of architectural styles. *Above:* The Mercantile Building was built in 1919 to house the first grocery store. Its parapet wall gives an almost western quality to the roof line while the wrought-iron trim lends a New Orleans feel. *Below:* Across the street the craftsman-style clapboard storefront of the Olde Naples Building has served as a bus depot, drugstore, movie theater, town hall, library, and post office. Built: 1921.
Photos, top: Jennifer Deane; bottom: Nanette Sanson.

Facing page: The historic Keewaydin Club on Key Island is accessible only by boat. It epitomizes the lure of the fishing lodge at its most elegant. Built with heartpine and stick-built materials and surrounded on three sides by water, the simplicity of its exterior camouflages its gracious interior. Built: 1935. Function and simplicity underlie the construction of these buildings. *Above:* The old Roberts Ranch bunkhouse blends into its surrounding landscape. *Below:* Hidden in an alleyway of Old Naples, garden plants climb the walls of a guest cottage.
Photos, facing page: Jennifer Deane; top: Oscar Thompson; bottom: Nanette Sanson.

Above and below: An outpost for arrival, the Smallwood Store bridges the gap
between land and sea. Inside, every rafter, nook, and cranny is filled with supplies.
Located on Chokoloskee Island in the Ten Thousand Islands this old general store
and Indian trading post is one of Southwest Florida's oldest standing buildings.
Built: 1906.
Photos: John T. Gillan.

The old post office in Ochopee is a favorite landmark for travelers passing through
Big Cypress National Preserve. Ageless in its simplicity, it measures only eight feet
four inches by seven feet three inches and is the smallest post office in the nation.
Photo: Kenneth White.

Above left: The Collier House on Marco Island, built in 1882, represents the historic tradition of the big front porch and the welcoming front steps. *Above right:* Homes, such as this artist's house and studio, line many of the waterways of the interior.
Their rustic style inspires a continual collection of artifacts of Florida lore.
Below: The charm and neighborhood spirit of Old Naples derives from the simplicity of design of its historic cottages. Along each street and alleyway, the mix of styles is gently masked by the march of trees, planted during the 1950s, that line each street.
Photos: top left and bottom: Nanette Sanson; top right: Ed Chappell Inc.

A touch of Europe brings the fantasy of the garden right up the walls of this home.
A simple structure becomes simultaneously domestic and fantastic.
Photo: Jennifer Deane.

Facing page and below left: This historic inland home, built in the craftsman style, contains a garden compound around which the main and guest houses sit. Architect of restoration: Andrea Clark Brown. *Above:* The earthy colors and textures of the Mediterranean style blend this home into its environment, on the cloistered quietude of the dunes. Architect: Steve Brisson. *Below right:* A bay-side home, designed in the Italian palazzo style, represents a more urban tradition softened by its sensitive relationship to the landscape. Architect: Al French.

Photos, facing page and bottom right: Jennifer Deane; top and bottom left: Nanette Sanson.

Previous page: The Venetian Villas in Park Shore are a playful allusion to a romantic
European precedent. This enormous housing estate appears to be a village grown up
over time through the use of color, style, and an almost dollhouse scale.
Architect: Walter Keller. Built: 1990. *Above:* The Bermuda tradition reiterates the
simple geometric shapes of cube and pyramid to form a light-filled home built of a
series of pavilions. Architect: Hugh Newell Jacobson.
Photos, previous page and above: Nanette Sanson

The residential building tradition constantly transforms and inspires innovations in building styles. *Above left and right:* Sitting atop the dunes of Marco Island is an unfettered display of European-inspired fantasy. *Below left and right:* A sanctuary of modernism is hidden behind the tradition of a stilt house facade. Designed by: Richard Geary. *Photos, top left and right: Nanette Sanson; bottom left and right: Ed Chappell Inc.*

Creating a balance between city and garden, these examples of commercial
architecture weave landscape seamlessly into the structure. *Clockwise:* The First
Union Bank is enveloped in vines, while the lines and curves of the Northern Trust
Bank Building are enhanced by the interplay of palm trees, and the geometric shapes
of the Hibiscus Center wrap around royal palms.
Photos, top left and right: Jennifer Deane; bottom: Nanette Sanson.

Color is a vital element in defining architectural detail and in rejuvenating many of the county's urban centers. *Clockwise:* In Naples, Tin City, Fifth Avenue, and Venetian Village are representative of small-scale buildings that have been given new life by the use of color, public art, and street furniture.
Photos, top: Jennifer Deane; bottom left: Carl J. Thome; bottom right: Nanette Sanson.

Above: A romantic illustration of pyramid steps and castle spires evokes a heraldic spirit in The Philharmonic Center's monumental shapes. *Below:* Large sculptural shapes interplay with the architecture of the Center's sculpture garden.
Facing page: In the lobby, the postmodern language of historically derived forms creates an elegant interior space. Architect: Eugene Aubrey, in collaboration with Forsythe Architects. Built: 1989.
Photos, top: Jennifer Deane; bottom: Nanette Sanson; facing page: Ed Chappell Inc.

ARTS & CULTURE

Collier County is one of the rare and fortunate places on Earth blessed with spectacular natural beauty, the rich cultural heritage of its Native American settlers, as well as a dedication to the enjoyment and promotion of art, dance, theater, and music. This love of the arts has fueled creative expression throughout the county for many decades.

The heritage of Southwest Florida's arts and culture began with the area's Native Americans. The colors and designs of their art work and the rhythms of their song and dance continue to delight audiences each season. From these early beginnings, the cultural experiences of early Collier County emerged.

Even when there was only one stoplight in Naples, there was an active cultural life. As early as 1951, the Naples Community Concert Association held performances in a high school auditorium before an audience of 1,500 subscribers; others not so fortunate were wait-listed for as long as four years to get seats.

Grace and beauty take motion as members of the Miami City Ballet prepare for a performance to be held at the Naples Philharmonic Center for the Arts.
Photo: John J. Gillan.

Theater also had its devotees. In 1953, the Naples Players showcased their first performances in a living room. They have been honing their skills and enlarging their audiences ever since—enough to warrant the construction of a new theater on 7th Street South by the end of this decade. In more recent years, new theater groups, such as the Pelican Theater Company and the Once-in-a-while-Park Players have joined the Naples Players in offering Collier County audiences a variety of theater fare including musical reviews, classical and contemporary comedies, dramas, and satires.

The Naples Art Association was launched in the mid-50s by three artists visiting on a front porch. Today the NAA's 640 members present regular art festivals, lecture series, workshops, and classes, as well as providing student scholarships in the arts.

The arts developed steadily over the next three decades. In the 1960s some of the area's first art galleries were opened in Old Naples. The public library was established in 1965, and, the Art League of Marco Island was started in 1969, launching the first of what is now the annual national Marco Island art show.

Free outdoor concerts by the Naples Concert Band began in 1973 in the Cambier Park bandshell in Naples. Today, its 78 members participate voluntarily for their personal growth and satisfaction. The Naples Concert Band and the Gulfcoast Big Band provide free concerts throughout the season at the park.

In 1978, the Collier County Museum was opened. Its displays, dioramas, and reenactments of the early periods of the "cracker" cowboy and Native American settlers bring the past to life. The museum also houses many artifacts from the early days of the Calusa Indians—the area's first inhabitants—unearthed in archeological digs on Marco Island and surrounding areas.

Another fine museum is the Smallwood Store in Chokoloskee, which was reopened in 1989 and is listed in the National Register of Historic Places. It is a restored trading post where Native Americans and early settlers once exchanged goods. The post contains many of the original wares which were traded during the early part of the century.

Many art organizations in Collier County thrive, due in part to the work of the United Arts Council—the county's designated local arts agency. The Council has acted as catalyst to educate, support, and promote the community's cultural life since its founding in 1980.

The Concert Association and the Fine Arts Society, along with the efforts of the United Arts Council, all helped to build an audience that would support a major arts center. When the Naples Philharmonic Center for the Arts was opened in November, 1989, the community, which had already demonstrated strong support for the arts, was ready to embrace a stage set for world-class presentations of the performing and visual arts.

The Philharmonic Center is home to an 85-piece symphonic ensemble, the Naples Philharmonic Orchestra, and the 86-voice Philharmonic Center Chorale. The building's marble foyer leads Hayes Hall audiences into art galleries and sculpture gardens, which share the facility. Since the Philharmonic Center's open-ing, more than a million tickets have been sold to people attending performances of international artists and companies such as violinist Itzhak Perlman, soprano Jessye Norman, London's Royal Philharmonic Orchestra, as well as big Broadway musicals including the Gershwins' smash hit, *Crazy for You*. A continuing education program in the arts, humanities, and sciences adds yet another dimension to the Philharmonic Center.

Collier County is known for its beauty, serene surroundings, and its love affair with its cultural heritage and with the arts. The diversity of this cultural experience continues to draw artists and visitors from around the world, assuring the ongoing growth of the arts community. From the earliest influences of Native American culture and art to the establishment of the stunning Philharmonic Center for the Arts, the arts have been a vital thread in defining the fabric of community life in Collier County.

Kris Paradis

Music resounds from Cambier Park throughout the year. The Naples Community
Orchestra strikes up free concerts under the baton of conductor Gale Waterland Scott.
Photo: Dan Wagner.

Above: The Naples Players, one of the area's most popular theater groups, present summer and winter performances of plays ranging from Neil Simon to Shakespeare.
Below: The National Very Special Arts program for the mentally and physically challenged is one of the many programs made possible by support from the United Arts Council.
Photos, top: Nanette Sanson; bottom: Tim Stamm.

Craftsman Dale Beatty brings the color and spirit of life in the subtropics to his art
while painter Paul Arsenault and photographer Clyde Butcher apply their talents to
documenting our architectural and natural heritage.
Photos, top left: Tim Stamm; top right: Nanette Sanson; facing page: Kenneth White.

Above: Preservation of heritage and honor of things past are brought to life in annual reenactments of the early Indian Trading Days at the Smallwood Store in Chokoloskee. *Below:* Seminole Indian art is a vital part of the tradition, tone, and character of Collier County.

Photos, top left: T. O'Keefe/Southern Stock; top right: John J. Gillan; bottom: Nanette Sanson.

The Civil War and "Florida cracker" cowboy periods are relived annually at the
Collier County Museum.
Photos, top left: Kimberly A. Bell; top right and bottom: Nanette Sanson.

Above: The rhythms and chanting of a Great Plains Indian dancer punctuates the annual American Indian Days Powwow ceremonies sponsored by the Seminole tribe.
Facing page: Artifacts of the early tribes of the lower Everglades have been unearthed on Marco Island and the Ten Thousand Islands. Many of these artifacts are on display at the Collier County Museum. The famous Marco Cat, depicted in this photograph, is now housed in the Smithsonian.
Photos, top: Cara L. Jones; facing page: William C. Minerich.

The internationally acclaimed Royal Winnipeg Ballet performs "Angels in the Architecture." Each year the Naples Philharmonic Center is host to many renowned dance companies.
Photo: Paul Martens.

Above: Big League Theatrical's 1994-1995 Tour of the *Secret Garden* is representative
of the fine Broadway productions that are performed at the Philharmonic Center.
Below: The Philharmonic Orchestra's annual "Holiday Pops" concert is a highlight of
the Christmas season.
Photos, top: Carl J. Thome; bottom: Nanette Sanson.

Marking the beginning of the holiday season, George Balanchine's *The Nutcracker*,
danced by the Miami City Ballet and accompanied by the Naples Philharmonic
Orchestra, is one of the Philharmonic Center's most important resident productions.
Photo: Nanette Sanson.

Collier County children perform with enthusiasm and poise their roles as the Little
Prince or Little Princess or any number of other roles in the annual performances of
the ballet, *The Nutcracker,* at the Philharmonic Center.
Photo: Eric Strachan.

Above: New educational opportunities at the Naples Philharmonic Center enable children to discover the thrill of the performing arts. *Below:* Maestro Erich Kunzel, known around the world as "the prince of pops," is the principal pops conductor of the Naples Philharmonic.
Photos, top: Lance Murphey; bottom: Nanette Sanson.

Sight and sound ignite to create a moment of magic as The Naples Philharmonic
Orchestra and chorale rehearse under the direction of Maestro Erich Kunzel.
Photo: John J. Gillan

N A T U R E

Collier County is an environmental jewel whose spectacular estuaries, wetlands, forests, barrier islands, and beaches form the natural infrastructure that maintains the region's sea life, water quality, plants and animals, and provides its scenic beauty. They also contribute immeasurably to the quality of life enjoyed by the residents of the region.

Thanks to farsighted conservation efforts in the past, nearly fifty percent of Collier County's land area is owned, conserved, and administered by private conservation organizations and state and federal agencies, ensuring that visitors and residents alike have many opportunities to see and learn about the area's subtropical ecosystems and native species. Exploring Collier County from inland regions to the Gulf of Mexico is a remarkable journey that courses from swamps to coastal estuaries, from mangroves to pinelands, and from grasslands to the beach.

Facing page: Sunrise paints the sky over the Everglades while a flock of great egrets begin their early morning search for food.
Photo: W. Metzen/Southern Stock.

NATURE

The mystery and beauty of the swamp can be experienced at the extraordinary 10,560-acre Corkscrew Swamp Sanctuary. Corkscrew encompasses dry and wet pine and scrub communities, wet prairie, marshes, lakes, and old-growth bald cypress forest, all visible from a two-mile boardwalk. This is the home of the world's largest remaining stand of mature bald cypress and the largest nesting colony of woodstorks in the U.S. Corkscrew is one of the region's best interior birding spots for species such as herons, egrets, woodpeckers, and hawks. It is also a habitat for black bears, bobcats, river otters, alligators, and turtles.

The 716,000-acre Big Cypress National Preserve is a major "ecological resevoir," containing wet prairie and dwarf cypress ecosystems as well as mixed hardwood swamps and young cypress stands. One of the most diverse natural regions in the county, the 61,962-acre Fakahatchee Strand State Preserve has a rich range of plant and animal communities. Here, fresh water drains from Big Cypress to the coastal mangroves of the Ten Thousand Islands through protected forested swamps. Mixed hardwood swamps, swamp lakes, wet prairies,

cypress domes, and hammocks are all found in the Fakahatchee, along with the largest stand of native royal palms in the nation.

With the Panther Wildlife Refuge, these preserves provide habitats for rare, threatened, and endangered species, including the Florida black bear, Florida panther, Everglades mink, and woodstork. They also act as natural reservoirs and pollutant filters. Fresh water flows from these inland regions to the coastal estuaries, bays, and barrier islands of the Gulf of Mexico.

Collier County's beautiful coastal ecosystems can be seen at the 12,000-acre Rookery Bay National Estuarine Research Reserve. A naturalist's paradise, Rookery Bay is a habitat for a variety of colonial waterbirds, shorebirds, ospreys, eagles, gopher tortoises, manatees, and bottle-nosed porpoises. The Briggs Nature Center, run by The Conservancy and located within the Reserve, provides information and public access. Here, scrub oak, pine and scrub, marsh, and mangrove ecosystems are visible from a half-mile long boardwalk and an observation tower. A new guided boat tour visits one of the Reserve's most recent acquisitions, North Key Island, a pristine barrier island and an important nesting area for loggerhead sea turtles.

Mangrove swamps converge with the only accessible tropical hardwood hammock in Southwest Florida at the 6,423-acre Collier Seminole State Park, which features a 13-mile long canoe trail along the Blackwater River, as well as an excellent one-mile long boardwalk and the start of the Florida Trail.

The Ten Thousand Islands, a maze of mangrove islands extending from Cape Romano, south of Marco Island to Cape Sable near Flamingo, is one of the most unique coastal wildernesses in the U.S. and one of the world's most extensive mangrove forests. This area supports a tremendous diversity of fish and wildlife, including sharks, rays, alligators, wading birds, eagles, ospreys, manatees, and dolphins.

These natural areas contain unique subtropical communities of native plants and animals linked together by watersheds and the Gulf Coast. Rich nearshore ecosystems, mangrove forests, and coastal barrier islands define the interface between the sea and the land. Incredibly productive coastal estuaries connect the land with the sea while very broad and shallow watersheds link inland wetlands, cypress swamps, and upland pine flatwood forests to the estuaries.

Temperate and tropical plant and animal species overlap in natural subtropical communities. Collier County, for example, is home to both the red maple, a species widely distributed through temperate United States and Canadian forests; and the gumbo-limbo tree, widely distributed throughout tropical Caribbean forests. Examples of animal species specially adapted for subtropical and tropical climates include the West Indian manatee, the Florida panther, and the loggerhead sea turtle.

Manatees, classified as endangered under the federal Endangered Species Act, graze on bay and estuarine sea grasses and must build up body fat to survive even the winter water temperatures in Naples. The Florida panther, a federally endangered subspecies restricted to Southwest Florida, occurs in pineland, hardwood hammock, and cypress swamp communities. Loggerhead sea turtles, named for their large heads, are a federally threatened species. These turtles spend most of their time at sea feeding upon crabs and mollusks. Only the mature females come to land to lay eggs in nests on sandy beaches from April to September.

Many native plant and animal species can be easily observed under natural conditions, giving even the casual observer a unique opportunity to appreciate the area's rich natural diversity firsthand.

Dr. John H. Fitch

The brilliant sunsets of Southwest Florida seem to transform the gentle waves and
white sands of the Gulf of Mexico into liquid gold.
Photo: Nanette Sanson.

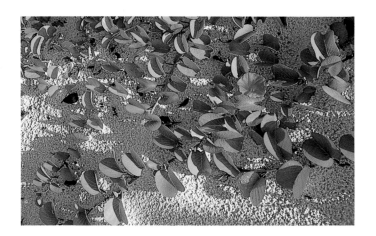

The patterns of nature are apparent in all forms of life found on the beach.
From top to bottom: Fiddler crabs scavenge for food; a railroad vine spreads across the
beach, helping to prevent erosion of the sands; a flock of royal terns falls into
formation at sunset.
Photos, top: William C. Minerich; center and bottom: Nanette Sanson.

Above: As the tide recedes, a nine-armed starfish, pulled back toward the sea, leaves only its impression behind in the sand. *Below:* A dusky damsel fish feeds on one of the sponge and coral reefs found in isolated areas off the shores of Naples and Marco Island. *Photos, top: Kenneth White; bottom: Rick Henderson.*

Brown pelicans and double-crested cormorants vie for a position to bask in the sun
after an early morning fishing expedition.
Photo: Nanette Sanson.

Above: As the sun rises, a flock of mature and immature white ibis forage in the cypress swamps off Janes Scenic Drive in the Fakahatchee Strand State Preserve.
Facing page: Southwest Florida also experiences a fall season. As young cypress lose their leaves, the forest in Fakahatchee Strand State Preserve seems like an unending sea of feathers.
Photos, facing page and above: Nanette Sanson.

The sight of a flower in the swamps and waterways can be both good and bad. *Above left:* The water hyacinth, introduced to Florida in the early 1900s, now threathens to clog many of the waterways. *Above right:* The pickerelweed helps to maintain surface water quality and is often planted when restoring or creating wetlands. *Below:* The anhinga or water turkey is a familiar sight along the waterways. Unlike most waterfowl, it has no natural water-shedding oils and must dry its feathers after diving for fish.
Photos, top left: Nanette Sanson; top right: Kris R. DeLaney; below: Connie Bransilver.

The mysterious and breathtaking diversity of vegetation and life forms in the
swamps of Big Cypress National Preserve reawaken in the spring. The cypresses bear
new leaves, the wild flowers begin to bloom, and the birds develop their full
breeding plumage as a new mating season begins.
Photo: Nanette Sanson.

An unusual assortment of birds of prey are found along the coast and in the forests of Collier County. *Above:* An osprey—a great fish catcher in the waterways of the mangrove islands—makes its nest atop a channel marker. *Center:* A bald eagle enjoys its afternoon catch. These majestic birds, whose numbers have greatly increased over the years, may be spotted from Naples to Marco Island. *Below:* The red-shouldered hawk is one of many bird species that may be seen in the forests of Collier County's preserves.
Photos, top: L.Lipsky/Southern Stock; center: Dick Cunningham; bottom: Rick Henderson.

Nature's palette of colors is applied with tropical flair throughout the swamps and forests. *Above:* This air plant is a member of the bromeliad family. While threatened with extinction, these plants are commonly seen hugging the trunks of cypress trees. *Center:* The colors and textures of lichen plants decorate the south-facing sides of cypress tree trunks. *Below:* Delicate and threatened butterfly orchids, found in cypress and mangrove swamps, were nearly wiped out during the freeze of 1989.

Photos, top: Nanette Sanson; center: Kimberly A. Bell; bottom: Kris R. DeLaney.

The roseate spoonbill is a rare and memorable sight, especially when it sports its breeding colors. Its diet of shrimp is responsible for its vibrant pink color, as well as for its presence in the southern estuaries of the county—major breeding grounds for Caribbean shrimp.
Photo: L. Lipsky/Southern Stock.

The prehistoric majesty of the alligator never ceases to fascinate. They can live more than
fifty years, eating only once or twice a week. Seemingly lethargic, they can move like
lightning, reaching speeds of more than 20 miles per hour for short distances on land.
Photo: Mia and Klaus.

Dressed in full breeding plumage, a great blue heron assumes a regal stance.
Inhabiting the entire seaboard, these herons grace our preserves year-round.
Photo: Nanette Sanson.

Above: Powerful and fast-moving storms streak across the Everglades in an almost daily procession during the wet season, replenishing the region with moisture for the upcoming dry season. *Below:* Fall brings early morning fogs, which blanket the marshes and cypress stands of Big Cypress National Preserve.
Photos, top: Kenneth White; bottom: Nanette Sanson.

Facing page: In spring, the cypress trees grow new leaves, forming a lacy canopy over a section of the two-mile long boardwalk at Corkscrew Swamp Sanctuary. *Above:* Blue flag irises dot the wet grasslands beyond the boardwalk. *Below:* Little blue herons are frequently seen fishing in the lettuce lakes of the sanctuary. *Photos, facing page: Kimberly A. Bell; top and bottom: Nanette Sanson.*

The forests of Collier County's preserves harbor a variety of animal life.
Above left: A white-tailed doe peers around a slash pine. *Above right:* The endangered
Florida black bear forages for food throughout the inland areas. *Below:* A bobcat is
released to help repopulate the species in the Big Cypress National Preserve.
Photos, top left and right: Eric Strachan; bottom: Lance Murphey.

Above: Pine flatwoods, typical of well-drained areas, are rapidly disappearing due to development. The ecosystem of many native plants and animals, the flatwoods represent one of the county's most threatened environments.
Following page: The dramatic and stark contrast of form and light in the Everglades echoes the struggle of this fragile wilderness to survive the encroachments of man upon this delicately balanced ecosystem.
Photos, top: Nanette Sanson; following page: Clyde Butcher.

Facing page: A red mangrove island appears to float in the distance. These islands
provide shelter and form the basis of the estuarine food web. *Above:* Woodstorks,
egrets, and herons congregate in the evening in the Ten Thousand Islands.
Below: The gentle manatee, a vegetarian, searches for food in the seagrass beds
found throughout the coastal areas of Collier County. The manatee eats up to 150
pounds of plants a day.
Photos, facing page: Oscar Thompson; top: W. Metzen/Southern Stock; bottom: Rick Henderson.

Sunsets off the coast of Southwest Florida are truly awe-inspiring. As the seasons
wear on, the colors become more vibrant and the patterns in the sky more glorious.
Photo: Nanette Sanson.

As the moon rises over Big Cypress, the mist brushes the light into subtle tones of color.
Photo: Kimberly A. Bell.

THE HEARTLAND

Beyond the bright beaches of the coast, in the direction of the rising sun, is a land that moves to a different rhythm. It is the heartland of Collier County. Increasingly squeezed between the protected regions of the Everglades and the edge of the city of Naples, this region is a world apart and as vital as a lifeline.

The names seem to drift from the past—Immokalee, Copeland, Ochopee, Everglades City, Chokoloskee, Caxambas, Goodland. So do the ways of life of farming, ranching, crabbing, and fishing.

More than anywhere else in Collier County, the heartland is a region where cultures meet and overlap, where myriad peoples are brought together by the drive for sustenance and the will to provide. It is also the abundant garden of Collier County. More than 1.3 billion tomatoes, enough to cover Marco Island completely, are grown annually, bringing in more than $100 million in revenue. A further $80 million derives from the marketing of vegetables such as peppers, cucumbers, squash,

Facing page: Laborers of nearly a dozen nationalities deliver a harvest that supplies
the majority of the United States with winter vegetables.
Photo: Mia & Klaus.

potatoes, and green beans. There is also the citrus fruit industry, worth over $35 million annually. Collier County produces more than 1.4 billion oranges, grapefruits, lemons, and limes each year. During the late winter and early spring, the heady scent of orange blossoms fills the air as the crop, enough to circle the globe three times, begins to ripen.

Consider, too, the ranchers and cowboys. In Collier County's not-so-long-ago past, the snap of their whips as they herded their cattle to market gave rise to the term "Florida cracker." Although the cattle are no longer free-ranging, the industry, which produces 6.5 million pounds of beef yearly, continues to thrive.

At the southern terminus of this fertile corridor, in the area around the Ten Thousand Islands and Everglades City, the scene is quietly changing as those who have made their living from the sea for over a century adapt to new conservation measures, including net bans.

Since the mid-1800s, when people first began to settle in these tempting but sometimes inhospitable lands, the pattern of lives built around the land and sea

has remained constant. The area around Chokoloskee and the Ten Thousand Islands was among the first to be settled but never really tamed. In those days, Everglades City was simply "Everglade," a rough-shod encampment of a few dozen pioneers.

Farming was the primary industry, and beautiful cabbages, beans, okra, and pineapples were grown and shipped to hungry but land-poor Key West. Sugar cane grew robustly without fertilizer. Soil analysis was simple but effective: if native vegetation grew, the spot was deemed fertile; if the produce did not taste salty, the soil was presumed good.

Eventually, fishing and crabbing industries were established by people living along and surrounded by the sea. Tomato-growing farms edged northward to Ochopee, the "Big Field," then to nearby Copeland. But it was in Immokalee (a name derived from the Seminole meaning "my home") that farming was destined to thrive, especially after access to western, eastern, and northern markets was ensured by a network of roads that sliced through the wilderness. Ranchers also moved in, attracted by the good grazing land for their cattle.

As land use has changed, so have the people and the cultures of those who live and work in these regions, resulting in an earth-toned rainbow of skin shades. Like those who came before them, these people face the challenge of not only building a good life, but also, of adapting to new surroundings while safeguarding the traditions and values that define their diverse cultures.

The first settlers in the heartland were the Seminoles and Miccosukees. These Native American tribes from Georgia and Alabama were pushed steadily down the Florida peninsula by ever-increasing numbers of white settlers. With their palm-thatch chickee huts and cypress canoes, native inhabitants established a hard but peaceful coexistence with a nature that exposed them to excessive heat, maddening mosquitoes, furious hurricanes, and stealthy alligators and panthers.

By adapting to the land, they were able to withstand without surrendering in the three wars waged against them by the U.S. government. But hot on their heels, always, came the white settlers searching for the last frontier. As befits a land where it is easy to hide, some came to escape previous indiscretions. Most, however, simply sought to carve out a self-supporting niche in an abundant land.

Such dreams of independence continue to sing the sirens' song. The unschooled or unskilled, the poor, and the hopeful have gravitated to the farms, ranches, and fishing fleets, hoping to find their own bounty in the annual harvest. Some come and drift on, following the growing season. Others find a means to settle in. Haitians, Mexicans, and Guatemalans are among those searching for a better life and a place in the sun. They bring with them the rich cultures of their ancestors.

As a result, a variety of traditions have taken deep root. Cinco de Mayo celebrations alternate with mullet festivals; Kwanzaa and the Green Corn Dance are marked as regularly as Christmas, making the heartland of plenty as rich in human culture as it is in natural life.

This is a region where nature's blessings are continually being sought and where life follows the rhythm of planting and harvesting. The hope in the heartland of Collier County is that the crops—a symbol of the enduring tie between human life and nature—will always grow resilient and strong.

Janina Birtolo

Successive frosts pushed the citrus belt south into Collier County, where groves were
first planted in 1965. Today, the county is one of the top citrus producers in the state.
Photo: Carl J. Thome.

Above and below right: Field laborers are paid by the piece and work at a breakneck
pace throughout the day, while packing plants run through the night.
Below left: The Mayans of Guatemala are particularly adept at harvesting the
palmetto bean, valued as a treatment for prostate cancer.
Photos, top: Kim Weimer; bottom left: Lucinda K. Hackney; bottom right: Carl J. Thome.

In this garden of plenty, the tomato is undisputed king. More than 1.3 billion are
produced annually. While much of the rest of the country sleeps through the winter,
Southwest Florida comes to bountiful life.
Photo: Kenneth White.

Tomatoes, peppers, and citrus—the region's three most important crops—create a
visual bouquet. Citrus and vegetables shape the economy of the county. More than
$250 million in agribusiness is generated each year.
Photos, left: Oscar Thompson; center: Mia & Klaus; right: Nanette Sanson.

A Haitian mother and child walk by a mural trumpeting Spanish-American
identities, a scene typical of the diverse cultural life found in Immokalee.
Photo: Kim Weimer.

Values that have long sustained Guatemalan ancestors
are honored by this family in their new home.
Photo: Lucinda K. Hackney.

The cultures and skin tones may vary but rich cultural traditions keep families
strong in Immokalee. Friends, family, and Immokalee social services provide
supporting elements that bridge the gap between the old ways and a new life.
Photos, top: Cara L. Jones; center and bottom: Lucinda K. Hackney.

Above right: Native Mexican traditions are still practiced as a young girl marks her entry into womanhood at her Quincinaro. *Above left and below:* Families and friends gather to celebrate at the Mexican festival of Cinco de Mayo.
Photos, top left: Eric Strachan; top right: Lucinda K. Hackney; bottom: Kim Weimer.

Chief O. B. Oceola and his son guide a dugout canoe through the Everglades, their homeland.
Photo: Carl J. Thome.

126

The Seminole elders still teach the old ways. The canoes, the clothes, and the chickee
huts are a way of life retained for practicality as well as identity in these wet, warm
environs. Every year, members of the tribe gather at Chokoloskee's Smallwood
Store/museum, where they celebrate the early trading days.
Photos, top left: Kim Weimer; bottom left: Cara L. Jones; right: Oscar Thompson.

Also important to the region are the contributions of ranchers and cowboys, who make use of lands not suitable for farming. Ranching captivates the young. With the guidance of 4H, a novice rancher can display his pride and joy at the Collier County Fair while down-home rodeos entertain everyone.

Photos, top: Lucinda K. Hackney; bottom: Eric Strachan; facing page: Penelope A. Taylor.

Like its leather trappings, ranch life wears well and endures in Immokalee. An early
morning roundup inaugurates the day.
Photo: Nanette Sanson.

The Wild West—Southwest Florida style—seems frozen in time at the Roberts
Ranch in Immokalee, one of the first successful ranches in the region.
Photos, top and bottom right: Oscar Thompson; bottom left: Nanette Sanson.

Above: Commercial fishing sculpts the tools, the faces, and the environment of towns such as Everglades City and Goodland. *Below:* Mullet fishermen once wound through the mangroves of Southwest Florida backwaters while dropping hundreds of feet of net. Net fishing was banned by legislation passed in 1994.
Photos, top: Oscar Thompson; bottom: Lucinda K. Hackney.

By the first light of day, a crabman is already at work loading his traps. The crab harvest is impatiently awaited each year by all lovers of this delicacy from the sea.
Photo: Eric Strachan.

OUR NATURAL HERITAGE

Within the thin, fragile band of water, land, and air that supports life on Earth lies a narrow subtropical zone of rich natural ecosystems sandwiched between temperate and tropical environments. Here, climatic conditions sustain life in one of its most productive and diverse states.

Only one region in the continental United States is included in this narrow subtropical zone: South Florida. Extending from Tampa across to West Palm Beach and south to the northern Keys, this zone is characterized by a rainy summer season and moderate winter temperatures with few hard freezes and magnificently diverse ecosystems.

The diversity of this realm reaches its apex in Collier County. Its low latitude ensures high average temperatures with rare frosts, and the peninsula shape exposes the entire region to maritime influences from the Gulf of Mexico, including high seasonal rainfall. The extremely flat topography not only promotes extensive wetlands, it also

Facing page: The continued existence of the wetlands of the Florida Everglades, already one-third their former size, is threatened by decreasing water supply, deteriorating water quality, and the rapid growth of non-indigenous plants, such as the melaleuca and Brazilian pepper.
Photo: Nanette Sanson.

causes the entire region to be flooded by relatively minor changes in sea level. Much of Collier County was submerged as recently as 4,000 years ago.

Since the land emerged from shallow seas, human beings have made their homes in these rich and lush surroundings. Centuries ago, bays and estuaries teeming with fish and shellfish attracted a variety of Native American peoples including the proud and warlike Calusas. Many settlers of European origin who moved into the area, however, strove to convert natural lands to grazing and cultivated lands. Many of the natural lands were drained, ditched, deforested, and planted with exotic species to convert them to "economically productive" uses.

The desire to tame this wilderness has had far-reaching consequences. Native species such as panthers, black bears, and loggerhead sea turtles have become endangered due to habitat destruction, mortality from collisions with automobiles, and from pollution. Still others, including the gentle manatee, are now endangered by boat traffic and the destruction of seagrass beds. The ghost orchid and other unique plant species were nearly loved to death by collectors for their rare beauty.

With the help of organizations such as The Conservancy, the Nature Conservancy, and the Florida and National Audubon Societies, however, residents of this extraordinary region have begun to realize that the biodiversity and environmental quality of native ecosystems and landscapes constitute invaluable social, economic, and aesthetic assets.

In Collier County today, semi-natural watersheds still convey water from inland swamps and wetlands to coastal estuaries and bays. Alligators have made a comeback. So have American bald eagles and ospreys. And, egrets and herons are no longer hunted for their plumes as they were earlier in the century. Roadside tunnels, installed so that wandering panthers may cross under major highways, are working as well. Nearly fifty percent of the land in the county has been put aside for conservation.

Slowly it is being understood that the "green infrastructure" of native ecosystems on which plants and animals depend is also necessary for the maintenance of human life. Collier County's unique environment is now seen as a trust from the past to be managed as a bequest to the future.

Dr. John H. Fitch

Encroaching civilization may render futile any efforts to restore the population of the beautiful Florida panther. With less than fifty breeding adults left, these unique predators may not survive the next decade without more habitat and the introduction of fresh breeding stock.

Photo: Lance Murphey.

Above: A summer intern at The Conservancy in Naples measures an adult female
loggerhead sea turtle that has just come ashore to construct her nest.
Below: A loggerhead hatchling rushes toward an uncertain fate in the Gulf of
Mexico. With luck and protection it may return in 30 years to breed on our shores.
Photos, top: Eric Strachan; bottom: Carolyn Colmer.

Above: The Moorings Park eagles begin the process of life's renewal. Successful efforts to control the use of DDT and to protect this majestic species from hunters have resulted in a resurgence of its population. *Below:* A young bald eagle, injured by a rifle, is released by a member of The Conservancy's Wildlife Rehabilitation Center.
Photos, top: William C. Minerich; bottom: Eric Strachan.

The sun sets over the mangrove forests of the Ten Thousand Islands Preserve. These islands are part of the largest wild subtropical estuary in the continental United States. This is the final step in a journey for these waters, which flow from Lake Okeechobee, through the Everglades' "River of Grass" and on to the Gulf of Mexico.
Photo: M. Bradley/Southern Stock.

Above: Pollution, entanglement with fishing lines, and loss of its natural habitat are
threatening the population of the brown pelican, our largest diving waterfowl.
Center: The widespread use of DDT almost annihilated these great fish catchers—
the ospreys. Today they are once again familiar residents of Collier County.
Below: Both elegant and comical, the roseate spoonbill is an increasingly rare sight along
Southwest Florida's coast, as its habitat becomes threatened by encroaching civilization.
Photos, top: Nanette Sanson; center: Kimberley A. Bell; bottom: L. Lipsky/Southern Stock.

These threatened wildflowers, all of which thrive in areas of wet prairie or wet pine flatwood, are among the more spectacular flowers found in Collier County. *From left to right:* the yellow batchelor's button, the grass pink orchid, and the catesby lily.
Photos: Kris R. Delaney.

Aquatic areas such as Big Cypress National Preserve, Corkscrew Swamp Sanctuary,
and Fakahatchee Strand State Preserve help to maintain water quality, as well as
providing habitat for the once rare and now common alligator.
Photo: W. Metzen/Southern Stock.

Above: The woodstork is the only stork native to North America. Its numbers have dwindled to endangered levels due to the loss of wetlands to development and water level changes related to ditching and dikes. Renowned for its quick reflex action, it fishes by touch rather than sight. *Below:* Manatees, already endangered from boating activities, which injure or kill dozens each year, suffer as well from the increasing pollution and loss of their primary feeding areas—the seagrass beds.

Photos, top: W. Metzen/Southern Stock; bottom: James Valentine.

Bird Island is typical of the timeless beauty and tranquility of Rookery Bay.
Photo: Ed Chappell Inc.

"No man is an island, entire of itself; every man is apiece of the continent, a part of the main..."

John Donne, 17th-century poet

The birth and growth of a mangrove island in the Rookery Bay National Estuarine Research Reserve is a lesson in the persistence and the fragility of natural ecosystems.

The miracle of life begins in a marriage between sea and land creatures. An oyster bed establishes itself on a shallow sand bar. Then a red mangrove seedling—from the plant that Native Americans call the "walking tree"—drifts by and settles to grow. Other drifting mangrove seedlings are caught on the roots of the first plant and take root. In time and under the right conditions, this mangrove expansion will create another island in Rookery Bay.

As the mangrove community expands, its branches offer roosting and nesting sites for herons, egrets, pelicans, ospreys, and other birds. The trees' root systems and shed-ding leaves provide shelter and nourishment for small fish and invertebrates. Indescribably rich and productive, red mangrove forests annually provide an estimated two tons per acre of organic matter as detrital food.

The mangrove island is just one example of nature's systems of fruitful interdependence. Southwest Florida's native plants and animals do not exist in isolation, nor do they randomly occur together. Instead, they exist in a "web of life," which is the product of thousands of years of evolutionary adaptation to one another and to the climate and chemistry of the ecosystems.

An estuary, forest, or other ecosystem depends on the natural community of interacting plants, animals, and bacteria, plus the chemical and physical characteristics of the surrounding environment. Sudden changes or the disappearance of key species can threaten the existence of many or all—just as a weak link can destroy a manmade chain.

Dr. John H. Fitch

CREATIVE CONTRIBUTION

CONTRIBUTING PHOTOGRAPHERS

Kimberly Ann Bell is a graphic artist and fine art photographer working in Ft. Myers, Fla. She displays her work at local art shows and is also owner of Portfolio Photographics, a stock photography agency.

Gilbert Booth is a commercial photographer living in Naples, Fla. While much of his time is spent fulfilling assignments for corporate clients and for portrait work, Mr. Booth continues to build his collection of aerial photography of Collier County.

Connie Bransilver is a freelance photographer residing in Naples, Fla. Her interest in the world's rain forests and the primates that inhabit them has taken her to many exotic locations, including the Tai Forest, Borneo, and Madagascar.

Clyde Butcher has been a fine art photographer for over 30 years. His work captures the fragile beauty of Florida's vanishing wild lands. His photographs hang in collections around the world and can be seen at his gallery in the Big Cypress National Preserve.

Ed Chappell has worked as an independent commercial photographer for 15 years. Based in Naples, he specializes in architectural and lifestyle photography. He is also owner of Aerial Ventures, an aerial photography service.

Carolyn Colmer has been a freelance photographer for over 15 years. She specializes in wedding and portrait photography at her studio in Naples, Fla. and enjoys nature photography as a special hobby.

Dick Cunningham is a nature photographer living in Naples, Fla. His nature and wildlife photography have been exhibited around the country, including several local galleries. He also runs Naples Custom Photo lab with his brother, Bill.

Jennifer Deane is a commercial photographer residing in Naples, Fla. She specializes in architectural photography. Her work appears frequently in local, regional, and national magazines.

Kris R. DeLaney is a botanist, photographer, and an expert on Peninsular Florida's endangered species of flora. Based in Sebring, Fla., he specializes in microphotography and has authored a number of scientific publications.

John J. Gillan is a commercial and fine art photographer from Miami, Fla. His work covers a wide range of subjects including architecture, landscapes, and Native Americans. Some of his achievements include the Historic Smallwood Store Traveling Exhibit and *Historic Architecture and Landscapes of Miami.*

Lucinda Kidd Hackney is a news and portrait photographer living in Naples, Fla. She has a degree in photojournalism from Arizona State University. Her work reflects her love for the scenery and diversity of the people found in the heartland of Collier County.

Rick Henderson is a freelance photographer living in Naples, Fla. For many years an underwater diving instructor, he now specializes in underwater photography, as well as nature photography.

Cara Jones is a photojournalist. After receiving her BFA degree in visual communications at Ohio University, she came to Naples and worked as a staff photographer for the *Naples Daily News.* She has since returned to the Midwest to continue her work.

Mia and Klaus, from Montreal, have worked together for many years producing some of Canada's finest scenic and nature photography. Over 15 books of their work have been published. Their photography has been featured in exhibitions around the world.

William C. Minerich has been an independent commercial photographer in Naples for nearly 20 years. He has received the Florida Degree of Photographic Excellence, Florida Service Award, and Master of Photography from the National PPA.

Lance Murphey is a staff photographer for the *Naples Daily News.* Prior to moving to Naples, he worked for United Press International in Denver and the Coeur d'Alene Press in North Idaho.

Nanette Sanson is a freelance photographer, photo editor, and stock photography production coordinator. After 13 years as owner of one of Canada's largest stock photo agencies, she decided to return full-time to photography and to publishing. She, subsequently, spent two years producing *In Portrait: Naples and Collier County* and establishing Profolio Editions Inc., a publishing company with offices in Naples, Fla. and Montreal, Quebec.

Southern Stock Photo Agency is based in Ft. Lauderdale, Fla. and represents over 100 photographers. While their files cover a wide range of subject matter, they specialize in nature, landscapes, and lifestyles of the Sunbelt regions.

Tim Stamm is a commercial photographer living in Naples, Fla. From food photography to architectural photography, his work covers a wide range of assignments and appears regularly in local and regional magazines.

Eric Strachan is director of photography for the *Naples Daily News.* He holds an associate science degree in photography.

Penelope Taylor is a freelance photographer residing in Naples, Fla. She specializes in wedding and portrait photography, but also enjoys photojournalism.

Carl Thome is a commercial/illustrative photographer. His studio is located in Naples, Fla. He has over 20 years of photographic experience in industrial, commercial, architectural, lifestyle, landscape, and portrait photography.

Oscar Thompson is a commercial photographer, specializing in architectural and scenic photography. A fifth-generation Floridian from Ft. Myers, his work has received many awards, including two Kodak International Snapshot awards and a Fuji Film Masterpiece Award.

James P. Valentine describes himself as "devoted to the stewardship of wilderness and wildlife," utilizing his talents as naturalist, photographer, and author to that end. He has published seven major large-format books on Southern landscape.

Dan Wagner is a photojournalist. He came to Naples to work as a staff photographer for the *Naples Daily News.* His work includes photography internships in Costa Rica and in India.

Kim Weimer is a staff photographer for the *Naples Daily News.* She holds a BFA degree in photography. Kim previously worked as a photojournalist in Philadelphia.

Kenneth White is an editorial and commercial photographer. Prior to relocating to Naples, Fla., he was a White House photographer for the State Department where he was the senior photographer for the Russian language magazine, *America Illustrated.*

CONTRIBUTING WRITERS

Janina Birtolo is a freelance writer from Naples, Fla. She has been writing for and editing publications for 15 years, including *Gulfshore Life, Home and Condo,* and *Traditions.* She is author of two historical one-act plays, which premiered in 1994 in Naples.

Andrea Clark Brown is owner and leading principal of the Naples-based firm, Andrea Clark Brown, Architects, P.A. Her award winning architectural design includes commercial, cultural, residential, and planning. She received the Prix de Rome from the Academy of Rome in 1979.

Rick Compton is a freelance writer living in Naples, Fla. His work appears regularly in regional publications and on public radio. He has received a Florida Magazine Association Charlie for excellence in writing.

Dr. John H. Fitch has been president of The Conservancy in Naples, Fla. since 1991. Over the past 25 years he has been affiliated with the Smithsonian Institution, the Massachusetts Audubon Society, Mainewatch Institute, and the Executive Office of President Carter as an environmental science advisor.

Kris Paradis is a freelance writer, editor, and advertising consultant living in Naples. She has written and edited for regional publications including *Gulfshore Life, Home and Condo,* and *Traditions.* She holds a masters degree in creative writing from the University of Louisville.

CONTRIBUTING EDITORS

Elizabeth Cameron is a travel editor, who lives and works in Montreal, Quebec. She has been working on travel books for the last three years.

Patricia Finlay is a freelance editor and writer living in Montreal, Quebec.

Nanette S. Sanson (see preceeding page)

DESIGNER

Jennifer Schumacher is president of Schumacher Design, an award-winning graphic design studio in Montreal, Quebec. She received her degree from Wittenberg University in Ohio and worked in New York City before moving to Montreal. Her family has vacationed annually in Southwest Florida since the early 1970s and now has a second home in Bonita Springs.

A FINAL WORD

The future of Southwest Florida is based in large measure on the degree to which we
appreciate, understand, and protect its natural and cultural beauty. Our efforts today
will determine if future generations will be able to live in and appreciate this
beautiful land as we do today.

Photo: Nanette Sanson.